PAY ATTENTION, IT'S IMPORTANT

WE NEED TO BE HERE NOW!

INDA PROCESS

BALBOA.PRESS
A DIVISION OF HAY HOUSE

Balboa Press books may be ordered through booksellers or by contacting:

Balboa Press
A Division of Hay House
1663 Liberty Drive
Bloomington, IN 47403
www.balboapress.com
844-682-1282

Interior Image Credit: Inda P.

Print information available on the last page.

ISBN: 979-8-7652-4450-0 (sc)
ISBN: 979-8-7652-4449-4 (e)

Library of Congress Control Number: 2023915676

Balboa Press rev. date: 08/23/2023

CONTENTS

INDA PROCESS

Inda Process was born in Philadelphia, Pennsylvania. She received a B.A. in Religious Studies from the University. Inda is a multimedia artist living in Arizona with her cat. Beginning her spiritual seeking in middle school with books by Swami Muktananda, she pursued the understanding of metaphysics at eighteen with the literature from the Church of Religious Science. Inda's personal recovery from alcoholism catapulted her into a lifelong seeking of God and the experiences of the mystics.

PREFACE

I thought about writing a memoir in the past couple of years, I was told I should by a Reverend friend of mine. When my Grandchild showed me a piece of art she created and titled, "Learning to Love My Old Soul," I was really moved. I said, "We need to write a book." I thought the writing would be about her (and her brother's) journey with homelessness. That didn't manifest because the teenagers (sister and brother) weren't able to communicate about their life experiences. I decided to tell <u>my</u> story of recovery from alcoholism and depression.

INTRODUCTION

I want to write about how I came out of the insane world of alcoholism. Being an adult child of alcoholics, I know from experience, how to take my personal pain and use it for good. If there are readers in this category, or are addicted, there is a way out. May this story suggest some hope to those who need to re-parent themselves, as I did. If so, I will be extremely grateful.

At "Adult Children of Alcoholics" meetings I learned that sharing is caring and necessary. It's a way out of isolation and all the anguish isolation brings. A burden shared is cut in half. Many of us become alcoholics ourselves to cope with a childhood or lifetime of abuse. These wounds may take a whole incarnation to heal.

I believe we come into this Earth school room to learn the soul lessons that will evolve us, whether we know it or not. You don't have to take my word for it. Finding a Higher Power, whatever you want to call It, will guide you on your spiritual path when you apply faith, willingness and honesty. Having an open mind is also a great tool for advancement. I believe all souls are full size. Applying the teachings of any religion can create the magnetism for miracles. The think it was Max Muller, a scholar, who wrote that the religions of the world have three things in common. There is a God, we're not it, and our Souls want to return home. Another teacher, Aldous Huxley taught people that the only corner of the universe you can be certain of improving is yourself.

Life now is so different from the days of turning my will and life over to alcohol. May my living the 12 Steps of recovery show another soul, how to learn to love and accept themselves. It took some time for me to feel deserving, but I made it. When I began trusting the home group and a Higher Power, that I didn't understand, I could go one day at a time without a drink or a drug.

Some may ask why I take such a risk to reveal the dark corners of my life. I was inspired by a quote in the Masterpiece Theater's show "Endeavor". The show airs on the PBS (Public Broadcasting Service) channel. Senior officer, Mr. Thursday asks the younger Investigator, Endeavor Morse, "Why do you stick your neck out like that?" Morse's reply, "because someone has too." Here's my story.

I grew up in an alcoholic home where there was a lot of physical hitting on each other. Yet, it wasn't all bad. We loved music and there was lots of Motown tunes and dancing in our small living room. There were many Sunday nights when we enjoyed ice cream cones in front of the black and white television set. We watched shows called "Lassie'" and The Ed Sullivan Show. I will never forget the first time we saw "The Beatles." My brother ran into the kitchen, where I was doing dishes and said, "hurry, you got to see these guys, they're gonna be big!" Us kids spent lots of time outdoors when the weather permitted. We had a nice sized back yard.

Mom nurtured roses in the far back of the yard and hedges surrounded the other two sides. There we played in the sunshine a lot. The beauty died as the family got sicker. Yet, my mother was a great cook. She could make a gourmet meal out of dirt, but we only got candy at Easter and Halloween. At Christmas, mom had a box of chocolates and I would help myself to them when no one was around.

As a small child I would go up to the front window of the third floor. We lived in a row house in a crowded neighborhood. There I would speak to God in the clouds. I'd ask for help for my mom and that dad would stop hurting her. I told my God I would be his helper and do what He wanted me to. Please, Jesus just make it stop. It didn't, things got worse.

There was a time when my oldest brother taped recorded dad beating mom. The screaming was horrific. My brother took the recorder to my dad's side of the bed.

I stood behind, watched my brother confront dad who listened to the recording. My dad wept. Alcoholism doesn't care if you're creating neurotic children and wives. I thought the domestic violence was a secret until the whole neighborhood got a look at the abuse right in front of our house. My dad was beating mother outside. I jumped on my dad's back to defend her, and tried to pull him off; but he flung me off like a piece of dirt. The police were called; dad spent the night in jail and came home the next day. Our lives were miserable. I didn't know that domestic violence was going on in other homes. I felt so depressed and ashamed. I wanted to shrink way inside myself where no one could find me. In a certain way, I believe I did.

Dad was not always an abuser. He was a war hero who served in Korea. He would tell us the story of how he crawled through the jungle with a bazooka on his shoulder and took out a tank. His unit could move forward and you could hear his pride when he spoke of it. Later he was the sole survivor of a jeep accident where the other four soldiers were killed. Dad had metals and a purple heart when he was flown home in a box of cotton; his neck and back broken. Everyone's life in my family changed with this accident. A good man would never be the same again. Family life went sour. Not many good memories were created since that time. There was a reason he got so messed up in the head but I believe he always loved us.

Sometimes when we'd call across the house, "mom, where are you? she'd say, "She died in Korea." War is not good for moms and other living things. We became alcoholics for a reason.

I had a lot of secrets, but there was a huge one I didn't talk about until I was eighteen. I did not speak of it again until I was in in my thirties, and then only when I was drunk.

School had been a safe haven, where adults smiled at you. I had straight A's and always had excellent grades. I decided to walk around the corner to get the homework assignments that I missed while I had the flu for a couple weeks. The gal I choose to visit was very quiet so, I thought it was a good idea at the time. Her father was something else, perhaps a sociopath, but definitely a pedophile. He took me upstairs to the third floor of the corner home and sat on a bed, where I started to cry so, he led me to another side of the room. Here is where I think an angel took me under it's wings. I don't remember anything else until he dragged me to the stairs. He laughed at me and said, "You can't tell anyone or I'll kill you and your family. I'll kill your family first so you won't have anyone to take care of you." The angel took me under it's loving presence again and I didn't come back to my body until I was on the ground floor and the girls that lived there were standing in a row. Like the Von Trapp family singers in "Sound of Music" they were standing straight but their mom was running from the front of the house to the back with her hands on her head loudly screaming, "No, No, Nooooo!" That family moved away somewhere.

I was walking home and just before I turned on to my street, I was back in my body again thinking, I can't tell my dad, he'll kill that guy and I won't ever see my dad again. My life was never the same. Another layer of shame. Another secret to keep to myself and more antenna invisibly growing out of my head. This world isn't safe anymore.

Years later, the whole third floor of that house was removed. I asked my mother if she knew anything about it. Her answer was, "the new owner said that the energy in there was very bad." No shit.

Disassociation #1

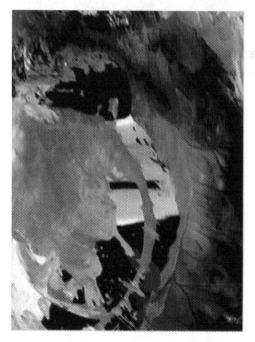

Disassociation #2

Not long after this, I had many stomach troubles and mom took me to see the doctor. I don't remember much from these visits except one time I heard the Doc tell mom that I should eat salad after the meal and not before. A much larger and more horrible crisis would happen soon after. It felt like living "The Nightmare on Elm Street."

Disassociation #3

I remember going to bed that night thinking, "it's too quiet." Like a premonition, it foretold of the most horrible event in my life. Dad stabbed mom in the throat with an army bayonet. I don't know how I got there but, I was in their bedroom alone with my mom, blood gushing out of her throat. I went next door and pounded on the door until my neighbor came and helped us. She guided me to put towels in the bathtub, ring them out and hold them to mom's open wound, so she could call an ambulance. Another angel experience or disassociation came upon me. I can't remember where I was or how much time went by. I came to, back in my body, when I heard one of my siblings say, "Mom is coming home from the hospital today."

Dad turned himself in to the police and I didn't see him for a long time. He went to prison. My sister told me that our fraternal grandmother took a sandwich to dad with a razor blade in it. The unthinkable happened and dad was found bleeding out. He was transferred to a mental hospital. When he was in the hospital he joined a recovery program. I'm not sure how long it was before his release. Mom came to school to announce dad's return. The principal came and got me out of class. I was thinking, what's up? When I got to his office, the news hit me really hard. I started to scream. He's a potential murderer! Why do you want him back in the house? I experienced more anxiety on top of the other major layers of shame that covered me. I didn't like who I was. I never brought friends home because I didn't know what to expect. The only time I liked my last name was when I had a brand new gym suit with my last name embroidered, in cursive, on the shoulder. The violence stopped and I saw lots of living amends being made.

Dad didn't hit my mother ever again. There were big jars of vitamins that came home with him and that he took daily. They seemed bigger than my head. Huge things that were supposed to help keep him healthy. He made amends to my mom and our family. It started by redecorating the home with new wall papering. Then painting the inside and the outside. It was a weird experience to watch him in a kind demeanor. I really didn't spend much time at home at that time. Us kids would go outside to play.

Mom paid for dad and us three youngest kids to go to Atlantic City. She grew up there. We learned what street mom lived on and that our granddad worked at the Ice Palace as a security guard. The boardwalk back then featured a horse that jumped into the ocean from a diving board. Wonders that were incredible for us kids.

The ocean proved to be a healing element; I don't remember much of the vacation. I was so afraid when I turned around and saw my dad kiss mom. It was a romantic kiss. I didn't like that. I saw my parents dance that weekend too. They were terrific! Jitterbugging in the back of the bar where we had dinner, this blew my mind. No alcohol was served. Could our lives really be free from it?

This was proof to me that my parents could have been happier before us kids came along. Mom had ten pregnancies and six children. There would have been seven, if my twin sister survived. She was born blue. I saw the death certificate which read, "dead on arrival." We were born at home on the couch. Mom told me that she was climbing the stairs to go to the toilet, but that was not happening. Back to the couch, here came the babies. Mother told me that she put me to her breast and I sucked right away. I figure that was my first drink because we were born on New Year's Eve. The neighbors came out with shots of whiskey ever year. Dad had a tax write-off fifteen minutes before the end of the year! I was told years later that my dad didn't want a lot of children, Oh, well.

I often think that we would have made great Buddhist. First precept, life is suffering. Suffering has a cause and there is a way out, the eight fold path.

At home, dad made me cheese and tomato sandwiches. Like baiting a dog, I came around, but I never fully trusted him again. Little did I know then that I would become like him. Alcohol proved to be a subtle foe. Candy is dandy, but liquor is quicker.

Although I started to get high in sixth grade I also was searching for answers to the crazy inner world I lived in. That summer I brought home stacks of books from the library. I think it was after I read a book by Swami Muktananda, "Thou Art That" I received some hope. Swami wrote, "God dwells in you as you." He was the guru of the Siddha Yoga path. At the age of fifteen he found his guru. I wasn't capable to understand what I was reading but I wanted Truth, something to make some sense of my life. I was only eleven years old. I decided to give the mantra a try.

I'd sit on the cement step of our row house and chant So Hum, I am that. It was suppose to help me with inner stability. I knew there was something wrong with me but I didn't know what it was. I wanted to control my thoughts. I fell in love with Spock, the character played by Leonard Nimoy in the TV series "Star Trek." I wanted the logic he talked about. There wasn't much of that in my world. Spock wasn't all human, so I guess that was his talent. I'm out of luck. Then, I fell in love with the vampire, "Barnabus Collins" in "Dark Shadows."

I remember being school smart but when it came to boys, I felt retarded. My picker was broken, like the woodpecker I saw continuing to peck on the cement street lamp. "It's not any good for you I want to shout. There's nothing for you there! Come on, find a tree will you? Not this unusual new thing without life." I heard a friend of mine say that she wanted to park this aspect of herself somewhere and drive away.

I can relate. I want to avoid pointing fingers at the guys that were in my life so I'll stick to my side of the story.

I wanted to feel better and to be happy. Getting high seemed like an easier softer way to relax and change my state of mind. It was very dangerous though. I guess I didn't care anymore what happened to my body, but I had to find something to relieve my anxiety for a little while. I tried to look good on the outside, but I was a wreck and suicidal.

I tried to run into a car in the evening, but was caught by the pharmacist at the corner drug store. He knelt down crying asking me to stop and go home. So, I did.

Later on, I found myself in the back of a big Yellow eighteen wheeler truck. I started out with a couple of friends to get loaded but woke up by myself. I crawled to the end of the open truck, like a soldier, and peered out. Good, I was in my neighborhood. I don't know how I got there but my clothes were on, good! There was another time when I passed out on the corner where we were hanging out. I had been drinking and someone escorted me home. I didn't know this until the next day when a neighbor told me that some guy found me around the block and carried me home. I am surprised that I am still alive sometimes. I have an awesome Higher Power!

God came into my life by way of nature. In the sixth grade, the same kid who taught me to sniff glue took me to Pennypack Park. I got off the bus and was in the forest in five minutes. I sucked up the energy from the trees like a sponge. My eyes were thrilled, my soul restored. Here, life was worth living. At last serenity. So I wanted to come back again and again. My inner light began to shine again with the lifting of a rock and finding a salamander. Like that salamander that I exposed, I became willing to totally expose myself to God in nature. I would be vulnerable and adore this world again. Thank you Creator for all the healing and good clean fun that my friends and I experienced there.

Today, I visualize lying in that grass in that open meadow. This image continues to be my safe place. I continue to go there in meditation for respite. I invite the spirits of rabbit, fawn, turtle, snake and even skunk. Native American spirituality has amazing attributes for each animal as a spirit guide.

There were trips to the psychiatrist before I was twenty years old. One doctor diagnosed me as having an anxiety neurosis. I forgot to tell him that I took a diet pill every morning and smoked weed, chased by beer each night. Now I see that the problem was of my own making.

I was first treated for alcoholism at a Mental Hospital. The problem was that I had an episode of being extremely jealous of my husband and his friend's, wife. I was sitting on the floor (we only had two chairs; we were poor), and I was drinking a can of beer. As they laughed and enjoyed smoking together, I got enraged and jumped up and pulled my husband down on the floor and started pounding on him. I behaved just like my father. I had blacked out and didn't know what I was doing. It was like being taken over by an invisible power and when the friend pulled me off of him I cried, to my husband, "please don't leave me, I'll get help." I began to forgive my father that day. When dad was sober he didn't abuse us. Alcohol did that.

I went to the Mental Hospital for outpatient treatment. They appointed a therapist that advised me to attend the church. He said he didn't want me to go to the "hole in the wall" AA Club (years later that AA Club is what saved my life). At the first counseling meeting, the counselor asked me how I drank. I told him I guzzled down one half of a can of beer, took a deep breath, then finished it off. He looked at me and said, "that's an alcoholic demeanor." The next question was, "do you black out?" Yes, was my answer, as I learned that black outs are a symptom of alcoholism. This progressive disease showed me that the first drink gets me drunk. I couldn't control how much I drank and where I would end up once I started. It was in AA that I learned of the phenomenon of craving, the physiological and cellular change that happens when an alcoholic imbibes. In my body, the cells screamed for more. I couldn't get enough and I always finished what I had and went to bed unless I could go out and get more.

He is in the big meeting in the sky now. I still appreciate how he was so encouraging. When I ran out of money for the counseling sessions, he invited me to have a sandwich at lunchtime. He showed me respect while we'd talk about the teachings at Church. Some say it was the beginning of the New Age movement. That church teaches about our oneness with God and that our use of the teachings of Jesus in our lives can transform our world. I could learn to experience the presence of God by meditation and prayer. I went to the church Library and devoured much of the literature from Unity Headquarters. The books by Myrtle and Charles Fillmore, co-founders of the Unity movement were life-changing and mind and heart expanding as well.

At the Sunday services I listened and concentrated on the lessons. I heard that changing consciousness could be attained by listening to classical music. I was on it. No more of the "I Can't Live, if Living is Without You." Songs like "Love has no Pride" and "I Can't Get No Satisfaction" were replaced with Mozart, Brahms and Bach. Of course, when I was with my family I listened to whatever their choices were. I had to change me and my thinking to a more positive, affirmative mind set. When songs were negative I would think cancel, cancel. They had a poster on the wall that read, "Bloom where you're Planted." That blew my mind. Really?

I remember when the Alcoholism counselor asked me if I thought I could forgive my husband, I said yes. But when he asked me if I could forgive myself, I sobbed. "No, I can't."

I am glad to report now that I have and do forgive myself for all the things that are objectionable. I didn't know what I didn't know back then. If I could have done better, I would have. I couldn't fight darkness with darkness. What I needed was light!

At church I was introduced to A Course in Miracles. The books from the Foundation of Inner Peace gave me a new way of walking, perceiving and looking with a different angle at my daily life. I took the lessons each day and meditated religiously with each one. I went to the evening classes where a group of us discussed how these new ways of looking at the world were being integrated in our lives. I had a really interesting experience one night as I drove to the A Course in Miracles class. I was frustrated as usual, egocentric and self centered. I was thinking about something I thought my husband did wrong when out of the blue I heard, "CARE!" This really shook me up and I timidly said, "ok." This voice was foreign and loud. It meant I had to spend the energy necessary for change. I couldn't remain the same any longer. There were other auditory messages that came to me years later, at a time I really needed them. I heard later on at AA meetings that this phenomenon happens often to people who are really ready to commit to change.

I joined the choir and got very active in the church. The choir members circled around one Sunday and told me that they loved me. I ran away from them. I didn't have any self-esteem. Some people come to recovery with low self-esteem, but I felt I had none. The song called "Let There Be Peace on Earth" at the end of the service cemented my desire to be there.

At a spiritual counseling appointment with the minister he told me, "Alcohol is a depressive drug, if you don't want to be depressed, stop drinking it." I did abstain from alcohol and I continued to get out patient therapy at the Mental Hospital.

I used subliminal tapes to relax with and to reprogram my subconscious mind. This happened to me around 1979. At that time, I did not know about AA meetings, but with the Bible, (a gift from a church) A Course in Miracles and the uplifting Sunday services, I remained dry. Spiritual growth came bit by bit. I was hungry for it and wanted to thrive.

I was a very angry woman without my crutch alcohol. A gal from the church asked me how I was doing and I lifted up the "One Day at a Time" daily meditation book and said with irritation, "I'm reading this everyday, that's how I'm doing.

When I showed up at choir practice a person anonymously gave me the text called, "Alcoholics Anonymous" and the book that explained the program of action called, "Twelve Steps and Traditions." I devoured these writings and added them to the already busy routine of reading the other spiritual literature I had acquired. Each morning before my son woke up I read and meditated as I was instructed. Over time I changed and became less of an ego maniac with an inferiority complex.

The counselor at Mental Hospital told me that alcoholism was hereditary. My father was definitely an alcoholic. So were his parents and siblings. I wanted to break the chain of abuse in my family life. I remained sober and had grown a lot when another disease struck our family.

When tragedy hit my family, (1985) I turned to alcohol again to cope. I didn't have a defense against the first drink. Someone handed me a beer and I started to drink it for medicinal reasons. I didn't get drunk at that time because I became my child's nurse.

Having reoccurring ear infections, my little one and I were directed to the hospital. The well baby doctor didn't see anything like this before. My son was diagnosed with leukemia when he was seventeen months old. Those doctors at the Medical Center told my husband

and I that they would do everything they could in their power to help, but sometimes leukemia finds a place to hide in the body and it could come back. They kindly said that it wasn't anything we did or did not do to cause it. My child had the kind of leukemia they usually found in old men. Chemo therapy took away the tumors that started to develop behind his eyes. We remained hopeful. Our love carried him to the end.

I was planning to be the bone marrow donor. The day I went in to the office for the blood test the doctor said, "I have good news and bad news. Good news first, you're pregnant. Bad news is you cannot be the donor for the bone marrow transplant."

I was a complete perfect match and so was my son who was 4 years older. My older son was too afraid to give the bone marrow when all the procedures were explained. They drill holes into your hips to remove bone marrow. Although there was one antigen off, my husband could be the donor. Since there was a doctor at Sloane Kettering Memorial hospital in Manhattan who knew how to do the procedure, that's where we ended up. My sick child needed lots of chemo therapy up to that time. Now, we travelled and stayed at the Ronald McDonald House. There the transplant was a complete success. How amazing it was to find out that the intelligence of the bone marrow knew what to do. It was placed in a blood bag and it was intravenously administered. Those cells went into the bone and began to grow the marrow. We did everything the doctor's asked. The doctors did everything they could. The leukemia did find a place to live after all those treatments, even 3 days of total body radiation. The cancer came back in December of 1985. My second child left his body on January 12th of 1986. I gave birth to our third child, a girl on January 23rd. It was at this time that God revealed Himself/Herself/Itself to me. Since I was preparing for a birth in twelve days, I was folding diapers to prepare. As I lifted the diapers in the chest of drawers, I sincerely said to my Higher Power,

"I know You didn't do this to me." At once I felt the wind, a spiritual gift of wind, around me, through me and blessing me. I thought my child was saying goodbye but now I believe it was the Holy Spirit saying, "Thank you." I had other God moments too.

The first day that my older son and husband went back to their regular lives, work and school, I had another spiritual gift given to me. I was walking from the bedroom to the kitchen when a "Readers Digest" magazine fell from the bookshelf right in front of me. I bent down to pick it up and it was opened to an article entitled, "Overcoming Grief, Bring Joy to the Living." Thank you God, Thank you God, in me. I kept the deceased's coat in the hall closet so that I could smother my face in it and smell him. I did that for a long time.

The death of my 2 year old son drove me insane, so I drank from 9 a. m. in the morning until I went to bed at night. I was functioning in a numb way. I had an infant to take care of, but I didn't want to feel my feelings. I found myself driving around with her in the backseat when I was under the influence. Another auditory blessing came and it said, "you just buried one baby, do you want to bury another?" It was maddening.

I tried to stop drinking but I couldn't. I called my minister and told him about the frustration and he said, "AA works for some people." A woman from the choir came and took me to my first Alcoholics Anonymous meeting at the AA Club. Since then, I am a sober member of AA for thirty six consecutive years. I was so mangled when I arrived, I surrendered and stayed. I'm powerless over alcohol and now I have a profound respect for what it can do to my soul, my body and mind. When the time came to feel those feelings, I was screaming into a pillow and it felt like I was putting my head in a lion's mouth and I would die. Many more treatments for anger followed and many classes on parenting too.

I took my feelings out on my older son. To make amends to him those amends had to be *living* amends. I went to Parents Anonymous every Wednesday night for a year and anger therapy once a week. My son and I had bunches of counseling. Grief counseling and parenting classes for me. I took the STEP parenting class twice because after two weeks, I started behaving poorly again. Then came the Nurturing Parent Classes. I enjoyed those classes but my older son was asked to leave. Oh well. He stayed home with his dad. What I am trying to convey is that life gets better when you work at it. It definitely gets different.

Aerobics were very beneficial. I woke up early before the children and jumped around in front of the television. I got lots of stuck energy out that way. I started to look better to. Self-esteem was developing rapidly because I was doing estimable things.

I made it a priority to be there for my now eight year old son. He (we) went through Cub Scouts for years - all the way to the "Arrow of Light." His grief counselor was driving beside us one day and got to see him in his uniform. My son and I joined 4H and had many years of completing classes on rifles, rock climbing, bee keeping and much more. Some of the classes allowed me to participate.

My friends have told me that our story has helped lots of people. I got sober even though my little boy went back to God before me. Some call it graduation. So, He graduated at the age of two. I bet he was an old soul. My deceased child asked me to be good to his brother the week before he transitioned. That was one of the last full sentences that he spoke. Such a tragedy, yet I am a more sympathetic and empathetic person now. I try to live AA's legacy of unity, service and recovery.

The lessons from A Course of Miracles were a comfort to me while the little guy went through the bone marrow transplant. I'd take my book and find a corner of the floor. I would call on the Holy Spirit and sometimes a warmth would come and cover me. I wasn't alone. ACIM helped me have a little peace of mind in between the fear of the transplant not working and his dying. Perhaps I was reading the Lesson, "I Rest in God."

Later on when I asked my first son, if he liked me better sober or drunk he said, "I like you sober, but I can't get any money out of you."

He came to me one day and asked why he was here (alive). I suppose siblings who have a deep grief ask this question. I immediately reminded him of the time he saved a little girl's life. The child was about three years old and was on a ride at the amusement park that looked safe for a little girl that age. It was a gentle by fun theme park ride that went around at a slow pace. This little one started to climb out of her seat and the frantic mom on the sideline started to yell and cry. I looked at my boy and said, "Go, get the baby." He did and he sat down with her until the ride stopped. My little hero climbed, while at a leisurely pace on an airplane ride that was moving. He rescued this frightened child of God and kept the mom from a nervous breakdown. I told him that our lives have meaning and he and I were here to help. I was so thankful that he accepted that answer. Even today he is described as kind.

Recently, (2023) my neighbor shared with me how many shootings there were since January, 2023. I couldn't and didn't want to believe. I'm an optimist, and tend to see the good in the world and in all of nature.

I don't know what prompted me to check the stats about the shootings, but I did. In four tenths of a second I saw there were one hundred and thirty six shootings since the beginning of this year. I lost it. Now, I see there have been many more since then. I felt like Howard Beale, a character played by Peter Finch in the 1976 movie "Network." I'm as mad as hell and I'm not gonna take it anymore! Fuming and distracted, I asked a friend for the name and phone number for a therapist. Since then, I've discharged some of that rage, but I am still pissed off. I need to deal with whatever is in my face. This news was so upsetting that I have to say to myself several times during the day, "Be Here Now, Pay Attention, It's Important!" I was driving down the road and could have hit someone if I didn't catch myself. Sometimes I wonder if I am able to *think* and drive anymore. That affirmation always brought me back to center and it's not working a potently as it did before.

In the past, it took more time to get news and information. We'd write a letter or wait to find the right book to look up statistics. I would wait for the eleven o'clock news. Now, with all the technology and the instant gratification, I can drive myself nuts in seconds. An invitation to insanity at my finger tips.

I was told that someone like me shouldn't watch the news everyday. There's no getting away from it. I get lots of information from my friends and even in the line of the grocery store. People are upset and vent in the most crowded places. I think "thanks for sharing and keeping me up to date with the crazy government trials and fake news." I think I see now why our world is ill and separated. I'm doing that thinking thing again Oh, well. There's tons of evidence why we're divided between us and them. I pray for peace on earth and let it begin with me and my attitudes. Can I choose peace in the mist of all this? It may not be easy but I will continue to try. My minister use to say, "When the tide comes in, all boats rise." That gives me hope because I attend lots of groups who want peace and health for our planet and all people. There is upliftment.

Fake news, these opinions aimed at damaging reputations and misleading the public, is another thing that really makes me mad. Be Here Now! Pay Attention! It's Important! There goes my brain with intrusive thoughts about the end of the world.

I named my inner critic Phyllis Diller when my therapist suggested I talk back to my negative self talk. Phyllis wasn't negative but a stand up comedienne. She created a character from hell. She was a pioneer in the industry of comedy but her laugh reminded me of my inner critic. I was tortured by it. As time when on I changed my inner nemesis name to the mean character in the movie, "One Hundred and One Dalmatians" - Cruella de Vil. She was not a nice person. Finally I named the saboteur Evillynn. Now I can laugh and tell myself Evillyn is acting up again. Simmer down now! Be Here now..you know the drill.

When I was a kid, my mom told me that we never tell another who we were voting for. That was private! Now we know exactly the political choices by reading the bummer stickers and signs in front of people lawns. I want to choose peace instead of separating myself from others. It is not easy at this time. Sensational head lines and negative character assassinations occur daily. It's important for me to pray for Divine healing for our world. It is scary to me.

I remember when my first son was in sixth grade and had an assignment to watch the evening news and report on a presidential debate. That's when, if you lost the election, you took it like a man. Following the debate a newscaster got on the screen to tell the people viewing what the candidate said. All I could think was how horrifying-that it is not what he said! While drawing the bath for my three your old daughter I asked her, "Who would you vote for honey?" She replied, "I'd vote for you mommy." Enough said. We are coming up on a presidential election soon so I pray I will not listen to opinions but the truth. I believe in Karma and Karma can be a bitch! Be Here Now, Pay Attention, It's Important!

Here are the steps I took, and take, to come out of the realm of anguish. I constantly need them to win the war of the wedge of doubt.

Step 1: I am powerless over alcohol, and my life has become unmanageable by me. (people, places, things and my life)

Although AA is a We program, and Most the steps start out with We, this book is about *my* using the 12 steps. Here is an example of just one of the unmanageable things I continued to do back then until it hurt too much.

I used to bounce checks for beer in the 1980's when floating checks was doable. My husband would scold me when I missed calculated and say, "Why don't you at least buy a case?" I suppose the penalty was about twenty-five dollars a check at that time. I was buying six packs because that was all I could carry as I pushed the stroller with my newborn daughter in it. Alcohol doesn't care if you have a new born. It's cunning, baffling and powerful. I wasn't falling down drunk, just comfortably numb.

I was ashamed of myself when I was scheduled to sing a solo at church and I didn't show up. I felt so awful. I was too hung over to go. I never behaved like that before (that I know of). It seemed like I didn't have a choice. A compulsion so strong was running the show. When I let go of something there are claw marks all over it. I cry "Uncle." Perhaps I need to do that with the news these days. News takes me places mentally that I don't want to go. I have to say to myself, "Be Here Now!" "Pay Attention!" "It's Important" to stop intrusive thoughts that don't feel good. Sometimes I find myself repeating that twenty times a day, maybe more.

One of my home group members said that drinking for an alcoholic is like dancing with a gorilla. It's not over until the gorilla says it's over.

A home group is a meeting that show you up to everyday or week. Some home groups meet once a week while others are daily. These people in my home group know what is going on in my life. There was someone who said, "even if you ass falls off, bring it to the meeting." My current home group is daily on zoom. One good thing that I'm grateful for since the pandemic (2020) is that I can go every day. Some of my sponsees (women I mentor) said that zoom meetings don't work for them; well it does for me.

There are lot's of different kinds of AA meetings and my home group has most of them. I'm talking about Big Book Study, Speaker meeting, Newcomer's meeting, Twelve Steps and Twelve Traditions Study, and an 11th Step meeting on Sunday. Sundays we meditate together and Saturday is our open discussion meeting.

Step 2: Came to believe that power, greater than myself could restore me to sanity. (AA.org)

There was something in the rooms of Alcoholics Anonymous that had an energy. I felt safe there and hoped that I could get sober and stay sober. Other people there had weeks, months and even years of sobriety. Each time I went up to the podium, in the front of the room, I was so proud of my and God's accomplishment. I could not stop on my own. Something was helping me, one day at a time.

I'm not in control of the world events and need to stay in my world of family, friends and therapy. Step 2 has given me permission to Let Go, Let God and crack my mind open to the idea there is a God - I'm not it. I don't know how to make things better in this world except by living the Spiritual Program of Alcoholics Anonymous and growing into the woman God wants me to be. Kindness to myself and others may look like taking myself off the hook, and accepting the things I cannot change. I don't like it, but acceptance doesn't mean I condone it, or want any part of it in my life. If I don't take care of myself, I won't be able to help my grand kids. They're the Light in my life right now, so is my cat. They need me as much as I need them.

Living the AA way of life gives purpose and meaning that I didn't have before. There have been too many coincidences for me not to believe. Is coincidence God's way of remaining anonymous? The more I let God or a Higher Power into my life – the more goodies I get. Not just the material things, but a sense that things will work out when I can't see a way for that to happen. I think that's faith. I can watch life like a movie and not get sucked in yet it is easier said than done. That took time. I use to butt in to people's conversations until a gal turn and looked me right in the eyes and said, "When I'm talking to him, that conversation is between me and him, you are not invited." Wow, Ouch, I woke up and heard her. Be here now, pay attention, It's important!

Step 3: I made a decision to turn my will and my life over to the care of God, as I understand God, praying only for the knowledge of God's will for me and the power to carry that out.

Every morning, before I'm get out of bed, I say, "thank you God for this wonderful day" even if it isn't a wonderful day. That sets a good attitude for the day and of course there will be days I can't do that. Other things get priority. Worry is the culprit. There's a 3rd Step Prayer from AA. Lord, I offer myself to Thee to do with me as Thou wilt. Relieve me of this bondage of self, so I may better do Thy will. When I turn my will and life over to God, I take my life out of the hands of the worry wort. Some people say, "If you pray, why worry? If you worry, why pray?" I'm not sure I truly get it, but I believe prayer brings me closer to my God. God is a bad word in the mouth of some alcoholics. I used G O D, Group of Drunks for a while. Here is a group of people that know how to live sober and I didn't know how to do that when I got to AA. When I came to the meetings of AA I had the gift of desperation (GOD). Some folks use Good Orderly Direction. I like all of them. My intellect doesn't take me to God. I'm told that the longest journey is from the head to the heart.

If I get mad at God I can jump right into Buddhism. You don't find the word God in the texts. There is an "Eight Fold Path." With good behavior you can achieve sobriety by discipline. Of course, there is no drinking alcohol. I find it very parallel to the AA program of action. Live with good conduct, right speech, effort, action, livelihood, mindfulness and no imbibing toxins and heal your mind, body and soul. Sounds simple, but not easy.

I saw a podcasts where David Bowie, one of my favorite musicians in the 1970's said, "Religion is for people who are afraid to go to hell, spiritually is for people who have already been there." Mr. Bowie had trained with a Buddhist teacher and was told this story of Chinese uprising. The teacher left his country with a couple of thousand monks and nuns. When they arrived at a safe country there were a couple hundred. That is hell!

Step 4: I made a searching and fearless inventory of myself.

Many people in the meeting rooms have said that they are afraid to do this step. They don't want anyone to know the terrible things that they did. Most of us have done worse. This step for me is an archaeology dig. I found out what makes me tick. It really is a path of self realization. Fear is the most dominant maladjustment that I have found. It disguises itself as all sorts of things. The Big Book of Alcoholics Anonymous says that there are a hundred forms of fear. I think there are lots more. Fear can also help keep me out of trouble too, so I pay attention.

It is a truly wonderful gift to get to the place where you can say, "It's OK to be who I am." I wouldn't hear those words until I was in my mid thirties. I was crying in the lunchroom and depressed as usual. One of my team members came in and said, "Hey, It's OK to be who you are."

I started to cry and realized that this woman was a great example of a happy woman for me. I sought out counselors most of my life but not one of them told me that. Eureka!

The beginning of the 4th Step was easy. First, I made a column of all the people I was mad at. Then the 2nd column, why I was mad. I was mad at a lot of people, places and things. The 3rd column asked me how this anger affects me. Is it my relationships, pocket book, Self esteem? The 4th column is where I wrote down my part in all the stuff I was complaining about. I had to ask myself was I dishonest, self-centered, self seeking or afraid? You bet I was afraid. Almost all the reasons that I got mad in the first place were because I was afraid of something. Sometimes fear disguises itself as anger and terror as rage. I could get so bent out of shape if the plans I made changed. I wasn't peaceful inside and I'd panic at first. I heard in a meeting that the only person that likes change is a baby with a dirty diaper. I was directed to work down the columns and not across. Working across created more anger.

Over the years I began to affirm that I am safe, it's just change. I had to have a bit of sober time to get to that place. One of the affirmations I cherish is "the past is dust, the future, now."

My sponsor tricked me one time by asking me to add the 5th column. Call it expectations she suggested, and just check it off. Wow, that inventory (I continually do them) showed that everything on my list at that time was an expectation. In meetings I hear that expectations are premeditated resentments. It's like drinking poison and hoping the other person will drop dead.

A Sponsor is someone who has worked the 12 steps of the Program of recovery. They have a Sponsor also. Many things can be explained with the help of someone who has read and worked the program of recovery. Did I mention that my sponsor was my brain for the first two years? I would call her with questions that I should have been able to answer myself, but I was all twisted up inside and couldn't think straight.

I remember the first time I was asked to sponsor. A woman approached me with eyes that were glazed over. I wonder if she was on Thorazine. I had to ask, "what happened?" She told me that her husband killed their children because they didn't have five fingers and five toes. I never saw her again. It was a postcard from God that read, "Stop feeling sorry for Yourself!" I had to give her credit for the willingness to ask. Sometimes, asking is too scary.

If my sponsor didn't know the answer to a question, she'd ask her sponsor. The relationships in AA are sometimes lifelong. If I have a burden there is usually someone who has experience, strength and hope about that situation. These people are my dearest Friends.

There were times when I had to lose and let go of acquaintances in the fellowship. My sponsor said, "We're not a hotbed of mental health!" Move on and so, I did.

In the Big Book of Alcoholics Anonymous, (called Big Book because of it's size when first printed) I read that resentments have the power to actually kill. More alcoholics pick up drinking again over resentments then any other reason. I can't afford resentments so what I needed to do was find a way to accept the people, places and things, I cannot change today.

The Serenity Prayer, part of Step 3 helped me a lot. God, Grant me the Serenity to accept the things I cannot change today, the Courage to change the things I can today and the Wisdom to know the difference today. I bring all my asking and accepting in the now. I heard that God meets us in the now, so I continue to say, "Be here now, pay attention, it's important." It's what it takes for me to get back to where my head, heart and ass are in the same chair.

Who am I to think that someone should be different than they are. I wouldn't want someone telling me how to live, except my Sponsor. She was my surrogate mom in early recovery. When she said jump, I wanted to know in what direction and how high. She had ten years of sobriety when I first heard her in a meeting. I choose her because in her story, she went into the recovery center in a wheelchair, but now, ten years later, she obtained ribbons of accomplishment, for horse riding. She had what I wanted. A Higher Power that Heals!

Covid-19 produced a lot of isolation. Isolation is dangerous for an alcoholic. I made it a priority to call three recovering women each day. I asked how they were doing. This is how I was trained in the first year, at AA.

I remember the sale of alcohol going up 200 % during the first month of the pandemic. I got the statistic from a website, so I'm not sure how truthful it is. The Center for Disease Control noted January 2020 as the date that the deadly pandemic was in full swing, worldwide. Shelves in the stores were emptying quick. I suppose drinkers didn't want to run out of alcoholic beverages, toilet paper was hard to come by too. I used all my tissues and started using the really good dinner napkins.

I read that the cost of alcoholism in our society is hardly estimable.

Step 5: I admitted to God, myself and another human being, the exact nature of my wrongs.

When I shared with my sponsor what I had written she said, "you never had anyone, did you?" I had to ask what she meant. She meant that I never had anyone to talk too when I was growing up and during those times of abuse and terror. That meant a lot to me. She was gentle and kind. I felt a relief that is indescribable. Like an empathetic vortex came into my aura. I got a lot off my chest and heart.

Wow, it is ok to be who I am. I hadn't had that feeling in a long time. The Big Book talks about how we can at last look the world in the eye, after finishing this step.

I heard in the AA meeting that secrets keep us sick. I want to be the best I can be. Confession in lots of religions is a very important. To unburden and clear the conscious. In AA, you're expected not to behave in the same manner again. It truly is a housecleaning.

My next door neighbor was a Saint. She showed me how to play cards, do find-a-word puzzles, play jacks and wall ball. We never spoke about the "Nightmare on Elm Street" episode. We didn't speak about any of it. My oldest sister mentioned to me once that she wondered why none of us got any help? I guess you didn't show your dirty laundry back then. Especially with all the blood on it.

Step 6: I became entirely ready to let God remove all my defects of character.

I got sober at a meeting place that had some rough characters. One person got up to the podium and said that the 6th and the 7th Steps were like a pick and a shovel. You can buy them at the hardware store but they don't come with instructions. "By God" he said, "You better learn how to use them."

In the Big Book of Alcoholics Anonymous, there are a couple of paragraphs regarding the 6th and 7th Steps, but the AA Twelve Steps and Twelve Traditions book has a chapter for each one.

I would call my sponsor irritated again, and she'd say, "Do a 4th Step and call me back." After years of this I would do the inventory first and then call her. I was a hard nut to crack.

There was a summer when my sponsor was out of the country, so I found another woman to work with me. Whenever I called upset she would say, "6 and 7." I also used this sponsor to do my sex inventory. It was sneaky but that's what I did. Most folks have one sponsor know all of their story. I was so ashamed of myself. I wanted love so much, I did some dumb things. Perhaps I was afraid of losing her love so I waited and told someone else the sex inventory. Learning to forgive myself has brought me to let go of the pain. I made mistakes but I am not a mistake. This earthly school room is rough sometimes. I can choose to not go back and re-injure myself. The past is dust, the future is now.

The Twelve and Twelve, as it's called is written by the co-founder to help the legacy and the groups to have an order and way to go into the future with a solid foundation. I am so glad that this literature is available because it helps me to navigate sobriety and sponsorship.

Step 7: I humbly asked God to remove my shortcomings.

Humility for me, is being teachable. I heard a woman share that in a meeting and I choose to keep that definition with me. I didn't feel comfortable in my skin, my life, and in my mind. I needed to be guided by the fellowship of AA and found that it's a Spiritual program, is an education without graduation. Step 7 is not easy. These steps are sometimes called simple steps for complicated people. I acted like a know it all a lot of the time. It caused troubles and I created a lot of situations that I needed to clean up. My ego is not my amigo. I heard that the ego speaks loudest and first. The more gentle voice is the one I can listen to for direction.

When I pray for the removal of feeling sorry for myself, I need to make a decision to not re-injure myself by dwelling and pondering the hurt feelings and the incident that cause the harm. I read we can become addicted to molecules of emotion. If there is an emotion we cannot stop, we may be addicted to it.

I can make a choice not to be a victim. Most of the time that I thought I was a victim, when really I was a volunteer. I set the ball rolling in the past and the outcome wasn't always pretty.

My sponsor taught me that when I get to the 6th and 7th Step with a particularly issue, I ask God to remove my shortcomings and place my mind where He/She/It would have it be. Then the difficult part of this step is to *act as if* God removed it, whatever *it* is. Over the years our relationship morphed into a situation that I didn't know if she'd love on me or metaphorically slap me upside the head. I gave her total permission, believe me.

One of my character defects was jealousy. As I grew in this spiritual program, I began to observe the jealousy coming up and I could stop my thought and say to myself, "God please remove this jealousy, and place my mind where you would have it be." The Big Book says, that at once we commence to outgrow whatever it is we asked to be removed. On this occasion it was my being jealous of women who had more money that I. Couples that looked happy at church, and quiet kids. Jealousy was a mask that my fear wore. I was able to overcome it by admitting, at a Spiritual Counseling appointment, that it was tormenting me. My minister said, "I just say to myself, I can do that, too." This advice proved to be a great gift.

I realized that for some of the things that I was jealous of, lots of material goods, money or prestige, I'd have to leave my marriage, my kids, and job to accomplish it. But, I could, if I chose to. The price was too great back then but, the jealousy began to evaporate. I also spent eighteen months asking that it be removed in my morning prayers. That's a long time ago, but I was so insecure all my life that it was worth all that effort.

Step 8: I made a list of all persons I had harmed and became willing to make amends to them all.

I used the 4th Step list because after processing and talking to another about the things on my list, I found I started the ball rolling most of the time. The problems were of my own making. I wanted what I wanted, and I created a mess because of it. I had to look at my part of the relationships with my parents, siblings and ex-husbands. I was married four times. Three were legal and one was a spiritual marriage. A woman approached me after a meeting one day and said, "Honey, you can sleep with them and you don't have to marry them."

Step 9: I made direct amends to such people wherever possible, except when to do so would injure them or others.

If I caused harm, I will apologize and not do that behavior again. If I owe money, I make arrangements to pay it back. If I broke something, I will replace it.

If I'm still very angry with the person, it's not time to make amends until I am calm. In doing this step, I used my sponsor a lot. I wrote out the things I thought I would say, and she read it and edited it. Most of the full page was crossed out and a few sentences were left. For instance, "I apologize for borrowing money and not paying it back. Here is what I will do to make that right. If there is anything else I have overlooked, please let me know." I was guided to write sentences that began with the word I. That way I wasn't finger pointing at the other person. I needed to clean my side of the street.

Sponsorship is important also for translation. I read the 9th Step promises and saw, "If we are painstaking in this phase of our development, we will be amazed before we are half way through." Oh no, more pain? My sponsor educated me that the word painstaking in this sentence meant steady progress. I was thankful for that. There were times too when my eyeballs were traveling across the page of the Big Book but my mind was traveling across the galaxy. It took a long time before my observer self could butt in and say, "Be Here Now, Pay Attention, It's important!"

Step 10: I continue to take personal inventory and when I'm wrong, promptly admit it.

At night, when I get into bed I ask myself was I dishonest or afraid? Do I owe an apology? Have I kept something to myself that should be shared with another at once? How could I have done better? After making this inquiry I ask God to let me know if there are any amends to make the next day.

This step reminds me that I need to be loving and tolerant to all. The Big Book has a chapter full of wisdom on this Step. It shows me how to be a better mom, wife, worker among workers, and a good friend. This maintenance step is a just one of the tools in the blueprint for living that I live now. I look at myself and take care of the moments so that God can take care of the day.

These days, I am also reminded to remember all the good that I did. Today I bought socks for my grand kids. I met with my sponsor and a friend in the program. We shared pictures of my grand kids and her nephew. That brought a lot of joy. I gave a ride to my grandson and his friends. I painted a watercolor. I suppose I had a good day!

Step 11: I sought through prayer and meditation to improve my conscious contact with God, as I understand God, praying only for knowledge of God's will for me and the power to carry that out.

When I started to try to meditate (1982) I used a tape, that my addictions counselor made for me. I'd lie down and listen to it and after a while, I relaxed more quickly. Detoxing from alcohol is not for candy asses. It's really hard. My body took a while to simmer down. I felt like a wild nerve wiggling around trying to find a life preserver.

I was working then as a bookkeeper. At lunch I found a couch across the campus of the University and claimed it. I was asked what I was doing there, so I told the truth. One woman who worked there actually took down the phone number of my therapist to have a tape created for her too. My tape guided me down the cellar steps of the home I grew up in. My dad was so scary and brutal when drunk, that my Mom and us three younger kids hid behind the steps in the coal bin. There weren't women shelters back then. My mom was adopted so sometimes we'd walk at night to Nanny's house.

So, each day when I listened, I visualized boxes floating out of the cellar from the coal bin. Words were written on them like fear, dread, unworthiness, and shame. I felt so much shame about my dad's disease and behavior until I found myself in the same boat. Alcoholism is a family disease.

I am truly grateful for my journey of recovery and the 11th Step.

I have become the woman I think my Higher Power wants me to be.

A Siddha Yoga master taught me that self effort and grace go hand and hand. (1989) One doesn't want to be without the other. She said that if you walk up to a water fountain and say, "I'm thirsty, give me a drink," you won't accomplish it. You need to bend down, turn the knob yourself, and drink the water. Just like two wings on a bird, she taught that we have to pay attention and to do our part to take good care of ourselves.

I learned that the benefits of meditation come after your practice. Sometimes, we don't notice for a while. When I judge that a meditation is really bad, too much thoughts going around or my inner critic has too much to say, "you're doing it all wrong," everything is totally all right. Intuition and hunches come, just when I need them. These are just a couple of the gifts of the practice. Staying calm when chaos is all around you is worth the effort to.

This morning I listened to church service on line. The chaplain offered a soothing meditation using the image of the ocean. She reminded us that on the surface there is a lot going on but, underneath is still and quiet. I followed her voice and experienced calm. Then, I used my magic magnifying mind to float in the ocean with a large surf board and sail. I welcomed a dolphin who smiled at me and we had a nice visit. I asked the water pal to pull my vessel and we slowly sailed across the top of the water. I became completely relaxed and happy. This journey took a few minutes and it's a golden nugget of the use of my imagination. I don't have to re-injure myself with traumas of the past. This is a new day and a new way of being. I love and appreciate myself. When my observer sees I need some help and healing, I now know what to do. Instead of impending doom, there's impending joy. I just have to reach for a better feeling thought.

Now, when I sit down to meditate, I usually sit in a chair. Some days I lie down on the couch or bed with a guided meditation from Ananda, playing on my phone. (Ananda.org)

As I begin, I take several deep breaths in, hold, and slow breaths out. These are the kind of thoughts I call to mind:

I am relaxed and appreciate the blood flowing in my veins. I breathe in love and breathe out fear. I am safe and secure in my ability to use my breath for self-healing and help. I call love (God) and help to me; I allow peace to flow into me.

I am grateful for my body and how well it works; for my stomach, assimilating nutrients and sending vitality throughout my body. I relax and allow involuntary functions to thrive. I applaud my hips, shoulders and wrists - all my joints are revitalized and strong. My body and Soul are integrated without fail.

I am attuned to my Higher Power and the Divine Teachers, Helpers and Guardians on the other side of this world. The cosmic realm of all possibilities is available to me and is the reason to sing songs of praise and joy. Grace comes to me in waves of salvation. I am grateful for the intuition that comes when I truly need it. I seek and welcome Conscious Contact with my Higher Power throughout the day and night.

Thank you, Lord, for my ears that heard the gentle support in the voices of the meditation teachers, for their magnetism that helped me go deeper into a splendid place within. Bravo God for sunrises and sunsets in the world and within me. Thank you for inner visions in the form of light, the healing wave pulsating and entertaining my consciousness. All is well.

<u>Step 12</u>: Having had an awakening as the results of these steps, I try to carry this message to alcoholics, and to practice these principles in all my affairs.

I continue to go to AA meetings everyday because that is where the newcomers are. I remember how that felt, and I usually go up to a new person and sincerely tell them, "we know how you feel." I have sponsored many women. Some stop working with me. I either worked the steps from the book with them too fast or too slow. God is in charge.

I feel, as a sponsor, my job is to direct women to the meetings, the literature and the Steps of recovery. We walk this spiritual road together. Sometimes I ask, "Are you asking for advice, or just venting?" Freely the time was given to me, so now I freely give. I usually give at least two hours to hear a gal's 5th Step. I usually tell of my experiences after their share to let them see we are in this together. Letting go of shame is huge gift of sobriety and the work.

I've had people ask me why I continue to go to meetings. Most people who stop going start drinking again. Today, I live in spiritual protection and grace, but early sobriety was different. I'd rather be curled up in a fetal position in bed, crying out to the God I couldn't understand, than drink again. To drink for me, is to die.

I had a sudden and frightening conscious contact with God. I had been meditating and practicing yoga for years. In those days, I was studying Hinduism and was serious about wanting to be closer to my Higher Power. The white Light that I experienced while sitting, was brighter than a thousand suns. I jumped up and got my journal. I wrote like a banshee. God had revealed Herself to me. I didn't tell anyone for a long time, but began to read, "The Autobiography of a Yogi" written by Paramhansa Yogananda. The book explained a lot for me. I was blessed with a cosmic gift. Even though I marveled at omnipresence, I was scared shitless. I believe now that I got these spectacular God shots to keep me on the path. This experience was overwhelming, but it let me know to keep doing what I'm doing. Later, I enjoyed studying other manifestations of the Almighty.

The story of Krishna (an incarnation of God) was profound for me. At the time of Krishna's birth, he was smuggled out of the prison his parents were locked in and exchanged with a new born girl. God created a lot of miracles to make this happen.

Krishna was the eighth son of Devaki. He was raised by the leader of the cowherds across the river. There was a good reason why.

The wicked King of Mathura, Kamsa (brother of Krishna's mother) heard the prophesy that Devaki's seventh son would slay him, so he murdered seven newborns. The new born girl was hurled against a rock because Kamsa didn't know the sex of his slayer. The baby turned into an eight-armed Goddess that said, "You're destroyer has already been born."

Devaki watched Kamsa smashed the skulls of seven newly born children. I took this story as another postcard from God, "Stop feeling sorry for yourself!"

I found prayer and affirmations to be powerful. These are the Prayers I use for Help and Healing from Unity Headquarters.

The Prayer for Protection by James Dillet Freeman

The light of God surrounds us;
The love of God enfolds us;
The power of God protects us;
The presence of God watches over us;
Wherever we are, God is!

The Prayer of Faith by Hannah More Kohaus

God is my help in every need;
God does my every hunger feed;
God walks beside me, guides my way
Through every moment of the day.
I now am wise, I now am true,
patient, kind and loving too.
All things I am, can do, and be
Through Christ, the Truth that is in me
God is my health, I can't be sick;
God is my strength, unfailing, quick;
God is my all; I know no fear,
Since God and love and Truth are here.

My favorite affirmation was "Everyday in every way, I'm getting better and better." That came from Yogananda. These affirmations seemed stupid at first. Then I found out that I had to put feelings to them to get the greatest benefits. The perceptual moments that brought about change in consciousness were many, after I tried this for awhile.

The artist in me created signs for newcomers that read, "Don't drink, Clean house, Help Others." I still see those signs in the living rooms of some of my closest friends.

So, to all of us who trudge the road to a happy destiny, all the best.

LIST OF SOME URL'S FOR 12 STEP RECOVERY PROGRAMS FROM:

Sober Nation - https://sobernation.com/list-of-12-step-programs

Alcoholics Anonymous – http://www.alcoholics-anonymous.org

Adult Children of Alcoholics – http://www.adultchildren.org/

For the Families of Alcoholics Al-Anon/Alateen – http://www.al-anon.alateen.org

Co-Dependents Anonymous – http://www.codependents.org/

Clutterers Anonymous – http://www.clutterersanonymous.net/

Emotions Anonymous – http://www.emotionsanonymous.org/

Food Addicts Anonymous – http://foodaddictsanonymous.org

Gamblers Anonymous – http://www.gamblersanonymous.org/

Narcotics Anonymous – http://www.na.org/

Nicotine Anonymous – http://www.nicotine-anonymous.org/

Overeaters Anonymous – http://www.oa.org/

Recovering Couples Anonymous – http://www.recovering-couples.org/

Sex and Love Addicts Anonymous – http://www.slaafws.org/

End notes

Grateful acknowledgment to the following organizations.

Alcoholics Anonymous World Services, Inc.
New York City

Unity World Headquarters
1901 NW Blue Parkway
Unity Village, MO 64065-0001

Profound appreciation to The Foundation of Inner Peace,
A Course in Miracles (1975) scribe Dr. Helen Schucman

About the Author 3rd person

This book distills the strength of a lifetime of personal struggle and ultimate victory. Over the years, I have heard her tell her stories three times and they never, ever vary. That is because THEY ARE TRUE. Take this loving woman's truth into your own sore heart and use it to help heal yourself.

Mariah H

It's interesting and rewarding to learn about one's journey through recovery, healing and wholeness. Inda's courage, faithful determination, tenacity and ability to be positive above and beyond circumstances is a gift. Sue Z.

ABOUT THE BOOK

This book is inspired by my granddaughter. She created a piece of artwork that was titled, 'Learning to Love My Old Soul." I was so touched by her expression that I said, "We need to write a book!"

Under the powerful art was written, "When I was adopted I struggled to love my past life and family and to let go of old things. Learning to love my old soul is me letting go and moving forward."

The insight is very parallel to my recovery process. I decided to share that process with the recovery world.

No one person speaks for AA. Within it's millions of members, each individual tells how he/she personally establishes a personal relationship with a Higher Power.

NOTES ON STEP 1

NOTES ON STEP 2

Notes on Step 3

Notes on Step 4

Notes on Step 5

NOTES ON STEP 6

NOTES ON STEP 7

NOTES ON STEP 9

Notes on Step 10

NOTES ON STEP 11

NOTES ON STEP 12

Printed in the United States
by Baker & Taylor Publisher Services